S0-AYS-929

EGYPTIAN MAZES

Dave Phillips

DOVER PUBLICATIONS, INC.

Mineola, New York

INTRODUCTION

WELCOME to a new collection of maze puzzles. This time we're traveling back to ancient Egypt and a civilization several *thousand* years old! This was an era of powerful pharaohs, countless gods and goddesses—many visualized with animal heads and human bodies—the finest solid-gold sculptures imaginable and immense stone monuments so cleverly designed that we still puzzle over the secrets of their construction.

Each one of these 36 mazes is based on an important part of the lore of ancient Egypt: a colossal statue, a mummy, a religious object, a bizarre animal god . . . . As you solve these puzzles, you will learn about the places, people, sights, customs and artifacts of a land that once ruled far and wide.

Remember that each maze has only *one* correct answer. For each, you must choose an entrance into the maze, pass *once only* through all the hieroglyphics or similar symbols shown in the puzzle, then end on the central illustration without retracing any paths.

With patience you should solve every maze, but if some defy your best efforts you may refer to the solutions on pages 37–45.

Copyright

Copyright © 1997 by Dave Phillips.
All rights reserved.

Bibliographical Note

Egyptian Mazes is a new work, first published by Dover Publications, Inc., in 1997.

International Standard Book Number

ISBN-13: 978-0-486-29658-6
ISBN-10: 0-486-29658-X

Manufactured in the United States by RR Donnelley
29658X08   2016
www.doverpublications.com

To find the one and only path to Queen Nefertiti's secret chamber, you'll need to proceed with extreme care. Enter the maze through the gateway on the right, pass *once* through the scarab symbol, then search out the special route to the queen. But don't retrace any path! (This world-famous painted limestone bust of the great beauty was discovered in the studio of an ancient Egyptian sculptor.)

The Colossi of Memnon at Thebes are statues of King Amenhotep III . . . and are *sixty* feet high. To reach their resting place, enter the maze from the upper-left corner, pass once through the hieroglyphic of the kneeling man, then find your way to those astonishing statues without retracing any path.

Some say that this Step Pyramid at Saqqarah, built for King Zoser in 2950 B.C., is the oldest stone building in the world. To reach it, enter the maze through the gateway on top, pass once through each hieroglyphic, then take that long journey to the site of this ancient building. But be careful not to retrace any path.

This bronze statue of the sacred bull Apis was found at the site of the ancient city of Memphis, on the great Nile River. To get a closer look, enter the maze from the top, pass once through each hieroglyphic, then find your way to the site of this holy figure without retracing your steps at any time!

This elaborate design was part of a decorative breastplate that belonged to an Egyptian princess. You can touch it only if you enter the maze at the top of the page, pass once through the den of each horned snake, then plot your path to the object without retracing your steps. There's only one route you can take.

This beautifully crafted model boat was built for King Tutankhamen's use . . . but in the *next* life! That's why it was placed in the tomb near the king's preserved body. You, too, can reach the secret tomb if you start at the top of the maze, find your way *once* through each bird's nest, then enter the boat chamber without retracing your path.

Notice the vivid scenes painted on this great gilded chest that was discovered in King Tutankhamen's tomb. They depict the great pharaoh's many fictitious battle victories. To get a closer look, wend your way down from the top, pass once through each hieroglyphic, then find a way to the chest without stepping down your chosen path more than *one* time.

Here's one of Egypt's most startling scenes—the four sculptures of Ramses II, guarding the Great Temple at Abu Simbel. The figures are immense, each one as high as a six-story building! This time, approach from the south, pass once through each of the four cane-shaped hieroglyphics, then choose a road to the Great Temple that never crosses back on itself.

There's one way—and one way only—to get close to this precious golden figurine of a seated pharaoh. (You know it's royal because he wears a crown and holds the crook and flail that symbolize kingship.) Once you enter the portal at the bottom, travel once through each of the four insect nests, then reach the pharaoh without retracing your chosen path.

How many workers do you suppose it took to drag this enormous royal sculpture?! Plenty!—if you believe this scene painted on an Egyptian tomb. If you want to help this mob, enter the maze, journey once through each little flowering space (there are four of them), then join the crowd . . . but don't retrace any steps you take.

Made from hippopotamus ivory, this boomerang-shaped wand was used to protect a sleeper from venomous night animals. Once you enter the maze, you'll have to traverse those four close-together insect nests (but once only for each nest), then find a way to the wand without ever crossing back on your path.

The symbol in the form of a stylized eye guards the one true path to the great Sphinx that has guarded Khafra's pyramid for over 4000 years. You'll need to find a way into the maze (this time, there are *two* possible entrances), pass once through that staring eye, then get close to the Sphinx without retracing your steps at any time.

Three ducks appear to be guarding Egypt's "Bent" Pyramid of King Snefru at Dahshur, so named because of its irregular angles—possibly a result of crack repairs in the steep walls of the original design. For a close-up inspection, enter the maze through one of the two portals, pass once through the "duck pond," then finish your trip without retracing your steps.

The cat had a special place in Egyptian lore, sometimes given godlike status. This one has been mummified, preparing its journey into the afterlife. To reach the cat's tomb, enter the maze (which door will you choose?), pass once through the space of each sharklike figure, then continue your search for the one and only path. (Remember not to retrace any steps.)

The Egyptian jackal god Anubis held a supreme position as lord of the dead—the inventor of embalming and supervisor of mummification (to preserve dead bodies for their voyage to the afterlife). Once you enter one of the two maze portals, pass once through each sawtooth design on your way to visit Anubis—but be careful not to cross back on whatever path you choose.

Here is a statuette of the goddess Isis caring for her baby Horus (whose father was the great Osiris, god of the underworld). For a closer look, choose an entrance into the maze and pass once through each *ankh*—the looped cross that was Egypt's sacred symbol of life. Then find the one and only path to Isis. As always, avoid retracing your steps.

For ancient Egyptians, this false tomb "door" (designed like a modern-day tombstone) was the passageway between the world of the living and the world of the dead. To reach it, enter the maze from either the left or the right side, step once only through each "foot" design, then search for the one and only path to the tomb site. But don't retrace your steps at any time!

This odd fellow is the dwarf god Bes, protector of children and pregnant women. He holds a Roman shield and a knife. To get a better look at him, enter the maze (left side? right side?), pass once through each tentlike hieroglyphic, then approach Bes by means of the only path to his domain—a one-way road with no turning back allowed!

Not every Egyptian pyramid was huge. Here's a small one—called a pyramidion—inspired by the great pyramids and built as a tomb for a respected private citizen—perhaps an official, a scribe or an artisan. If you want to get near this structure, find the one correct way into the maze, pass once through each of the guardian figures, then wend your way carefully to the pyramidion without retracing your steps.

Yet another figure with an animal head and a human body! Wearing a cobra on her lion's head, this one is Wadjit, goddess of Lower Egypt. To meet her in person, find your way from one of the two maze entrances, then pass once through each "A"-shaped design. As you hasten along your chosen path into her personal chamber, remember that retracing your steps is *not* allowed!

Here is a finely detailed picture of the sacred *ankh* first seen on page 16. Only kings, queens and gods of ancient Egypt were permitted to carry this powerful symbol of life. Two scales of life flank the *ankh*. Once you're in the maze (which door will you choose?), you'll have to pass once through each scale as you puzzle out your intricate road into the large central space. But be careful not to go back on any step you take.

Deadly asps guard the single road to the site of this Egyptian obelisk—a structure sacred to the sun god, Re (and a model for America's Washington Monument). Pointed pillars such as this one were traditionally covered with hieroglyphic writing describing the victories and achievements of kings. To reach it, pick a doorway into the maze, journey (quickly!) through each snake pit, then seek the unique path to the sacred site without ever backing up.

Bastet, the Egyptian goddess of music and dance, was symbolized as a cat or a cat-headed woman. To seek her bronze statue, enter the maze through one of the two gateways, go once through each bird cage, then find the hidden path to the central space without retracing your steps at any time.

Here is the high priest Amenwashu kneeling before a stele—an engraved stone slab inscribed with praise for one of the numerous Egyptian gods. You can get a close-up look at the inscriptions if you choose the correct doorway into the maze, pass once through each snakelike design, then seek the one, true path to the center (a hidden route that can't be retraced).

The Great Pyramid, built by King Khufu (called Cheops by the Greeks), is the largest stone structure ever built, covering 13 acres at its base. It is thought to be about 4000 years old. The king's tomb was found deep inside the limestone pyramid, at the bottom of a steep, stone-filled shaft. To reach this site, enter the maze through one of the bottom gateways, pass once through each hypnotic eye, then select the only correct route to the pyramid itself. But never retrace your steps!

Here, carved in slate, is one of ancient Egypt's most famous couples: the beloved King Menkaure and his sister-wife Queen Khamerernebti II. It is he who built the third, and smallest, of the three Pyramids of Giza. To reach the main chamber, enter the maze (right? left?), pass *once* through each of the four guardian dogs, then wend your way along the one good path to the waiting royalty. (Don't forget that you can't retrace any steps you take.)

Here's a closer look at the inscriptions carved on a stele—that stone slab we first saw on page 24. Following traditional practice, it was inscribed with hieroglyphics in praise of one of the many gods of ancient Egypt. Enter left or right (only *one* door will lead you onto the good path), pass once through each of the four pitchers, then try to discover the only route that will take you directly to the stele. Remember that once you choose a path, you can't retrace your steps.

King Tutankhamen's special fame stems from the sensational discovery, in 1922, of his lost tomb, the ornate richness of his *three* golden coffins, the wealth of objects crammed into his tomb; and also from his youth: for King "Tut" was only 18 when he died. This statuette shows him spear-hunting, possibly for a hippopotamus. If you'd like to join him, choose one of the two entrances to the maze, pass once through each of the four bird cages, then find the one and only path to the central space. Don't retrace your steps.

Here's a sample of young King Tutankhamen's glorious treasures: his famous death mask, magnificently crafted in burnished gold. To get a closer look, choose either the left or right gateway into the maze, pass once through each of the four bird chambers, then find the unique route that will lead you to the mask without once retracing your steps.

Seti I is thought by many scholars to have been the greatest king of his time—1300 years before Christ. His burial place is the finest in the Valley of the Tombs of Kings at Thebes. To see his mummy—shown here surrounded by its linen wrappings—choose the correct entrance, pass once through each rabbit hutch, then find the true route (there's only one) to the burial chamber. Remember never to go back over your steps.

The three Great Pyramids of Giza are the oldest of the Seven Wonders of the World. All were burial sites for Egyptian kings, intended to bring about a closer union between heaven and the deceased ruler. To visit this famous site—shown here surrounded by smaller *mastabas*—pick the correct door into the maze (for the first time in this book there are *three* to choose from). Then pass once through each fish chamber as you try to find the single correct path to the pyramids. And no retracing of steps allowed!

The god Thoth was held by the ancient Egyptians to be the inventor of writing, the creator of languages and adviser of the gods. Thoth is represented here in human form, with the head of an ibis, one of his sacred animals. With *three* gateways to choose from, enter the maze, pass once only through each serpent's den, then search for the one and only avenue that will reach mighty Thoth. Don't retrace your steps.

Four gateways to reach King Tut!!! But only *one* is the right way into the maze. Once you find it, pass once through each star chamber, then locate the true road to this life-size statue of Tutankhamen. It was made for his spirit to inhabit in case anything happened to his body. (Remember not to retrace any path you take.)

Horemheb was an army commander before he became king of Egypt in 1348 B.C. Here, built in his honor, is the Colonnade of Horemheb, formed by huge pillars at the Temple of Luxor. To reach this mighty edifice on the bank of the Nile River, begin your trip at one of the four corners of the maze. Then pass once through the two cross-shaped hieroglyphics. There's only *one* good road . . . and you'll have to plot your way to the site without retracing your steps.

Horus, son of the mighty Osiris and originally the god of Lower Egypt, is always represented as a falcon or a falcon-headed male figure. Here, the falcon god is perched atop a pole that once held a flag. To enter his central space, choose one of the four gateways into the maze, pass once through each ibis (those long-billed birds), then locate the single correct path to Horus' perch.

Better skip this one if you don't like beetles! For this adventure, you must choose an entrance into the maze (only *one* of the four is good), pass once through each scarab nest (don't get bitten . . . there are *six* nests to navigate!), then locate the true road to Tutankhamen's stunning gold coffin cover.

SOLUTIONS

Page 1

Page 2

Page 3

Page 4

Page 5

Page 6

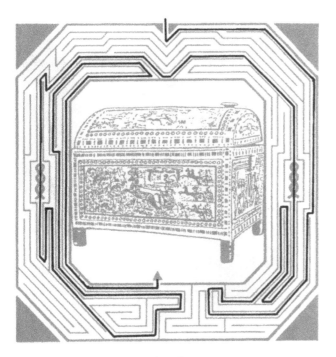

Page 7

Page 8

Page 9

Page 10

Page 11

Page 12

Page 13

Page 14

Page 15

Page 16

40

Page 17

Page 18

Page 19

Page 20

Page 21

Page 22

Page 23

Page 24

Page 25

Page 26

Page 27

Page 28

Page 29

Page 30

Page 31

Page 32

Page 33

Page 34

Page 35

Page 36